MASTERS OF MOTION

HOW TO FLY THE SPACE SHUTTLE

RUSSELL SHORTO

ILLUSTRATED BY GREGORY TRUETT SMITH AND CHRIS BRIGMAN
PHOTOGRAPHY BY EDWARD KEATING

Acknowledgments

We would like to thank Jeff Carr and Rob Kelso of NASA for their active and generous support of this project.

John Muir Publications, P.O. Box 613, Santa Fe, NM 87504

First edition. First printing December 1992

Library of Congress Cataloging-in-Publication Data
Shorto, Russell.
   How to fly the space shuttle / Russell Shorto ; illustrated by
Gregory Truett Smith and Chris Brigman ; photography by
Edward Keating.
      p.   cm. — (Masters of motion)
   Includes index.
   Summary: Explains how space shuttles work and what astronauts do
during the course of a shuttle mission.
   ISBN 1-56261-063-5
   1. Spac shuttles—Piloting—Juvenile literature. 2. Manned space
flight—Juvenile literature. 3. Discovery (Spacecraft)—Juvenile
literature.   [1. Space shuttles. 2. Astronautics.] I. Smith,
Gregory Truett, ill. II. Brigman, Chris, ill. III. Keating, Edward, ill.
IV. Title. V. Series.
TL795.5.S5   1992
629.44'1'0973—dc20   92-19014
                                                                    CIP
                                                                    AC

Consultants: Agincourt Press
Design: Ken Wilson
Illustrations: Gregory Truett Smith, Chris Brigman
Typography: Ken Wilson
Printer: Worzalla
Photographs by Edward Keating,except as follows: photographs on
pages 2 (both), 3, 6-7, 8, 8-9, 9, 13, 14, 16, 20, 21, 25, 26, 27, 28, 33, 34, 35,
36, 39, and 42 courtesy of NASA; photograph on page 11 courtesy of
Honeywell; photograph on page 23 courtesy of Lieber Labs; and photo-
graph on page 30 courtesy of TRW, Inc.
Drawing on page 31 courtesy of TRW, Inc.; drawing on page 32 courtesy
of NASA.

Distributed to the book trade by   Distributed to the education market by
W.W. Norton, Inc.   The Wright Group
New York, New York   19201 120th Avenue NE
                                         Bothell, WA 98011

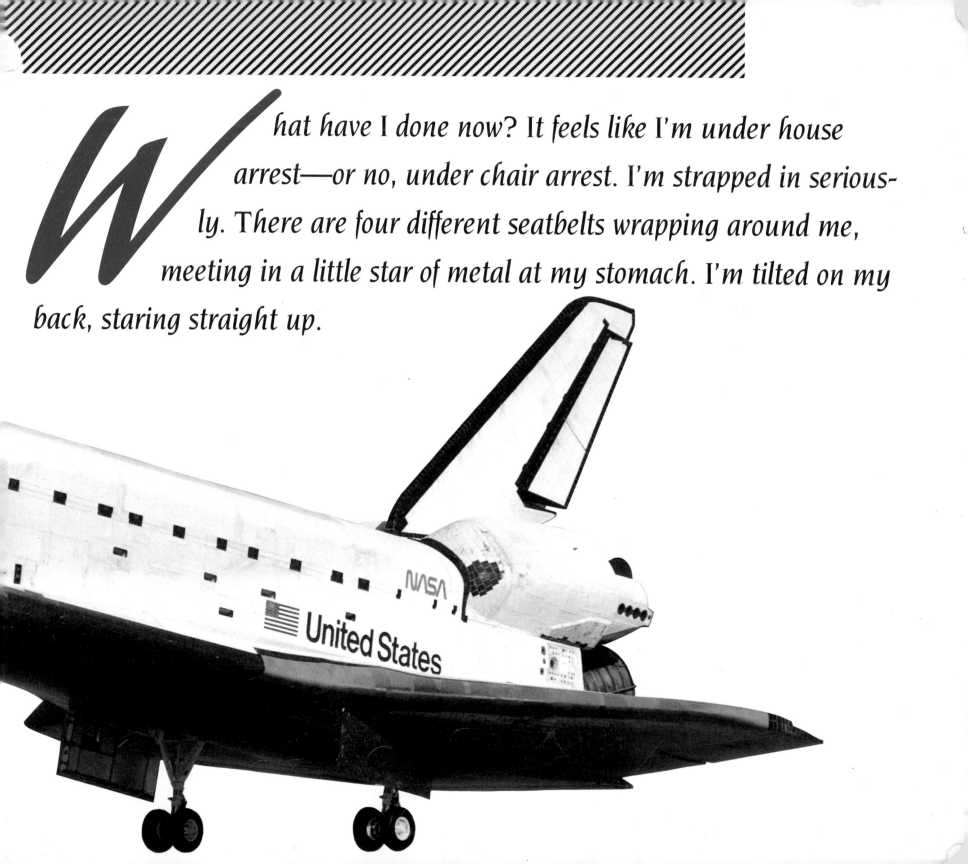

What have I done now? It feels like I'm under house arrest—or no, under chair arrest. I'm strapped in seriously. There are four different seatbelts wrapping around me, meeting in a little star of metal at my stomach. I'm tilted on my back, staring straight up.

There's a panel of switches and a small computer screen in front of me. Actually, there are controls all around: thousands of switches, knobs, dials, and buttons. Is this some kind of high-tech torture chamber? I'm about to scream, "I confess! I'll tell you whatever you want!" when I hear a man's voice crackling in my ear.

T *minus thirty seconds and counting.*

I look to my right. There's a guy sitting there, also staring straight up. He's dressed in a bulky orange suit and wearing a helmet. He nods and gives me a little salute. I look to my left. Out the window I see bright morning sunlight and a tower.

"Hey, what's going on?"

"Don't worry," the man answers. "Just wait for the launch and be ready to work the procedures."

"Launch? Procedures? Where am I? Who are you?"

"You're on the space shuttle Discovery. Call me Pilot or PLT. You're Commander or CDR. We go by titles here."

"Commander? Me? You've got to be kidding." The first voice breaks in again.

Discovery, KSC, we're at T *minus twenty seconds and counting.*

Pilot answers, "Roger, KSC." Then he turns to me. "You're supposed to say that."

"Oh, sorry," I say. Then an obvious question pops into my head. "Hey, what happens in twenty seconds, anyway?"

MISSION CONTROL

It takes more than just the crew aboard the orbiter to run a space shuttle mission. At any given time while the shuttle is aloft, it is being monitored by a team of no less than 80 experts who work at the Johnson Space Center in Houston. Three of these teams work in shifts around the clock, for a total of 240 ground controllers.

For organizational reasons, the ground controllers are grouped into departments, with each department overseeing different aspects of the shuttle. For example, the Guidance, Navigation, and Control Systems department takes care of those systems, while Flight Dynamics is responsible for orbital adjustment

maneuvers, and Payloads is in charge of the cargo scheduled to be deployed on that mission.

All the department chiefs report to the flight director, who is the sole authority for each shuttle mission. Flight will listen to the recommendations of the mission experts, but he or she alone makes the final decisions. For example, if a main engine fails during an ascent, Flight decides whether or not to continue the mission. If a computer malfunctions while the shuttle is in orbit, Flight decides how to deal with the situation.

But Flight never talks directly to the shuttle's commander. Instead, all communications go through the spacecraft communicator, called CAPCOM. (This title is a holdover from the early days of the space program, when mission astronauts rode in capsules.) When Flight makes a decision, he or she tells CAPCOM, who relays the order to the shuttle's crew. CAPCOM is always an astronaut, because astronauts are so familiar with the shuttle and its crew that they know the best and fastest ways to get the information across.

FLIGHT DECK

MID DECK

CHIPS

EQUIPMENT BAY

H₂O SUPPLY

"Liftoff, of course."

It takes a minute for that to sink in. "Umm, I just remembered a very important appointment with my tree surgeon. So if you don't mind, I'll be leaving now."

"Ordinarily that would be fine with me. But do you have any idea how many millions of taxpayer dollars it would cost to halt the launch at this stage? Just sit tight and prepare for liftoff."

I take stock of the situation. I've always wanted to go into space, but this is a bit sudden. Is it a nightmare or a dream come true? There's no time to think.

T *minus ten seconds and counting. Nine, eight, seven...*

"Hey, Pilot. If I'm the commander, is there anything I'm supposed to do? I mean, am I supposed to press some buttons or flip some switches? How will the engines start?" Just as I say this, I feel a rush of rumbling energy. Clearly, the engines have started without my help.

"Oh, don't worry," says Pilot. "The shuttle's computers took over operation at thirty-one seconds before launch. They're running the show now."

"Well, that's a relief."

Three, two, one...liftoff!

INSIDE & OUTSIDE

The space shuttle has three primary components: the solid rocket boosters, called SRBs; the external fuel tank, called the ET; and the orbiter.

Each of the two SRBs stands 149 feet tall, just 2 feet shorter than the Statue of Liberty, and contains 1.1 million pounds of fuel. The SRBs provide the main power—a total of 3.3 million pounds of thrust—for lifting the shuttle off the launchpad. They are also equipped with parachutes, which enable them to float safely back to earth. Once the SRBs land in the Atlantic Ocean, they are retrieved by special ships for eventual reuse.

The ET carries the fuel that powers the shuttle's main engines. It stands 154 feet high and contains 385,265 gallons of liquid hydrogen and 143,351 gallons of liquid oxygen in two separate tanks. The ET is released about eight and a half minutes after liftoff, once the shuttle's main engines have been cut off and are no longer needed. It is not reused.

The orbiter is the most versatile air vehicle ever made. It takes off like a rocket, flies like a spaceship, and lands like an airplane. The main sections are the crew compartment and the payload bay. The crew compartment has three levels. At the top is the flight deck, where the commander and pilot monitor the flight. The next level is the mid deck, where the crew sleeps, relaxes, and performs experiments. At the bottom is the equipment bay, where equipment, trash, and the water supply are stored.

MAIN COMPONENTS

CREW COMPARTMENT

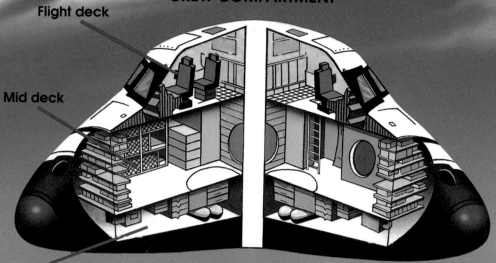

Flight deck

Mid deck

Equipment bay

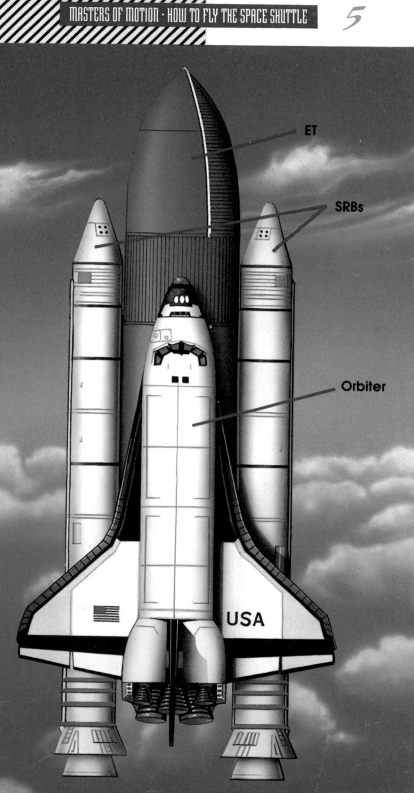

ET

SRBs

Orbiter

USA

FLIGHT DECK

LIFTOFF

The rumbling that I've felt for the past few seconds suddenly becomes an avalanche as a tremendous force thrusts us upward. I look out the window and watch the tower slip away as we crawl past it, seemingly in slow motion. The entire cockpit starts to shake now—and me with it. My teeth feel like they're going to rattle loose. I have this incredible urge to push my foot to the floor, as if doing that will brake this thing. Pilot says something into his microphone about a "roll" program. Then a new voice comes over my earphones—a woman's voice.

Roger, roll Discovery!

"Who was that?" I ask Pilot. But before he can answer, the voice comes again.

Discovery, Houston. You're go at throttle up.

"Hey," I shout through the roar, "I think you've got the wrong number."

"Don't be silly," says Pilot. "That's CAPCOM. Tell her we're go at throttle up."

"But I don't know what that means."

"Just say it."

I shrug. "Roger, Houston, we're go at throttle up," I say into the microphone, trying to keep a calm tone.

"Good work," says Pilot. "We'll get you through this yet."

We're flying upside down now, but it doesn't seem that way on the flight deck because the force of our acceleration is pushing me back against my seat. I can hear the wind whistling furiously as we power through the atmosphere.

Then we seem to go into high gear. An invisible hand pushes my whole body even farther back against the seat as the shuttle streaks ahead. I've been on a lot of amusement park rides in my day, but this is intense.

"WEEEEEEEEEEE!"

"Try to be a little more professional, Commander," Pilot shouts over the noise. "And stop flapping your arms around."

"Oh, right. Sorry. But this is pretty cool. What just happened? Did we put the pedal to the metal?"

"That's exactly what we did. You see, the same forces that power us through the atmosphere also put a lot of stress on the vehicle. About twenty-five seconds after launch, we have to throttle down to relieve that stress. Then, once the pull of the earth's gravity

THE CREW MONITORS:

SPEED

HEADING

FUEL CONSUMPTION

KSC is in charge of preparations for shuttle missions up to and including liftoff. As soon as we clear the tower, the Johnson Space Center in Houston takes over. CAPCOM is the communications officer there."

"Hmmm. I'm still a little confused about exactly who is running this mission. I would have thought the commander was in charge, but it seems as though CAPCOM is really top dog."

"No, CAPCOM just relays orders. The flight director in Houston, whom we astronauts call Flight, is the chief authority. But if you're asking who flies the shuttle, the answer is none of the above. It's really the computers that do the hard work."

"So we just sit back and enjoy the ride, I guess."

"Well, no. Our main job at this point is monitoring—making sure everything is going according to plan. If a slipup occurs, we have to take action."

Discovery, Houston, com check.

I put my hand over the microphone and turn to Pilot. "What does that mean?"

"It means they're checking in with us. They want to make sure our communications equipment is working properly."

I adjust my microphone. "Roger, Houston. We read you loud and clear."

Pilot reaches over and taps me on the shoulder. "Excellent." Suddenly I hear a small

eases, the computers automatically throttle up again."

"In other words, we have to slow down or else we'd break apart?"

"Something like that."

"Another question: Who is this woman called CAPCOM, and what happened to the first guy?"

"The first voice was KSC—the Kennedy Space Center in Florida, where we took off.

Commander's flight deck panel

but unmistakable explosion. The incredible rumbling lets up, and a great rush of energy washes over me, as though a weight has been lifted from my shoulders. "What happened?" I ask Pilot.

"That was SRB sep," Pilot says to me. "SRB stands for solid rocket booster. The boosters are the long, thin tanks that were attached to us on the launchpad. They were responsible for helping get us off the ground, but now they've done their job, and we just released them. 'SRB sep' means the solid rocket boosters have separated from the shuttle."

"Oh, I see." The ride is much smoother now, and I'm starting to feel a bit more relaxed. Not having much else to do at the moment, I peruse the bewildering instrument panel in front of me. "Hey, Pilot, tell me about these indicators."

Pilot leans over and points. "That's the altitude scale," he says, pointing to a gauge on the console in front of me. "It shows you that we're now 30 miles above the launch site. And this one next to it, marked ALT RATE, tells you that we're moving at 4,200 feet per second, or about 2,900 miles per hour."

"That's faster than a speeding bullet."

"Oh, it's nothing. Once we leave the earth's atmosphere, you'll really see some movement."

Discovery Houston, two engine TAL.

I turn to Pilot. "What was that about?"

"It's just an abort capability call. It means we can lose an engine and still be able to land in Spain by dinnertime."

"Sorry, you lost me there. What does Spain have to do with losing an engine?"

"A number of landing strips around the world have been designated as emergency landing sites in the event of a major problem in the shuttle's ascent. One of the primary sites is in Zaragoza, Spain. If, say, we lost an engine at this point, CAPCOM would call for a TAL, or Transatlantic Landing abort. The base in Spain would be alerted, and we'd fly across the ocean like an airplane."

Discovery, Houston, all engines operating at 104 percent.

I give Pilot another confused look. He frowns and takes over my job, saying, "Roger, Houston. All engines, 104 percent."

"How can the engines be operating at more than 100 percent?"

"CAPCOM doesn't mean 104 percent of their capacity. Nothing can operate at more than 100 percent of its capacity. What she means is

FLIGHT DECK

This G meter measures the force of acceleration.

104 percent of the power they were putting out at liftoff. Mission Control has determined that 104 percent of liftoff burn is the optimum level of engine power for driving the shuttle through the atmosphere efficiently. In other words, the engines are putting out 4 percent more power now than they were at liftoff."

I lie back against my seat for a minute. I've been noticing a strange sensation coming over me, and it has suddenly gotten much stronger. I can't move my head, and my arm feels like there's a 20-pound weight attached to it. I also notice that I'm having trouble breathing. Struggling, I finally manage to bring my left arm up to my chin. Then I push my helmet to the side so I can look at Pilot. "Hey," I gasp, "I think something very

ACCELERATION

Acceleration is an increase in speed. Inside a car traveling at a constant speed, the passengers don't feel any sensation of movement. To them, aside from the occasional bump, the car seems to be at rest. When a vehicle's speed increases quickly, however, such as when the space shuttle's engines go "throttle up," the force of the acceleration is so great that it pushes the passengers back in their seats. When the shuttle throttles down, or slows its acceleration, the astronauts inside feel as though the orbiter has come to a complete stop.

weird is happening."

"It's the g forces. We're moving at 3 g's now, which means that our acceleration is exerting a force equal to three times the earth's gravity. Your arms are heavy because they weigh three times what you're used to."

"O.K., I can live with that—for a while, anyway. What's the next stage?"

"We're due for MECO in about two minutes. That's NASA talk for main engine cutoff."

"You mean we're going to turn off the main engines in two minutes?"

"I thought I just said that."

"But won't we fall?"

"The main engines power us through the earth's atmosphere. But once we approach orbit, we don't need them anymore. Out in space, we only need engine power for maneuvering, and we've got two separate systems for that—the orbital maneuvering system, or OMS, and the reaction control system, or RCS."

"Why not use just one type of engine?"

"Because we need different levels of thrust, just as craftsmen need different tools for

ROCKET POWER

Rocket power may seem like a very modern invention, but in fact the first rockets were probably built in the thirteenth century, possibly in China. A rocket is any projectile that contains its own fuel and has a source of oxygen available to burn that fuel. Typically, the oxygen is found in the surrounding air. When the fuel and this oxygen combine, an explosion takes place. The force of that explosion drives the projectile forward.

For centuries, rockets were used as weapons and fireworks and for communications, but the scientific principle behind them wasn't fully understood until Isaac Newton formulated his laws of motion in 1687. Whenever a force is applied in one direction, Newton wrote, an equal and opposite force will also be generated. If igniting a rocket's fuel causes the fuel to explode downward, for example, then an equal and opposite force will send the rocket upward. In other words, for every action, there is an equal and opposite reaction.

Recently, the most important figure in rocketry has been Robert Goddard. Goddard's dream was to build rockets that could leave the earth's atmosphere and fly in outer space. But there was a problem: there is no oxygen in the vacuum of space. So Goddard had to figure out a way for his rockets to burn their fuel once they left the atmosphere. He solved this problem by equipping experimental rockets with their own supply of oxygen in the form of a liquid oxidizer that could be carried along with the fuel. Goddard died in 1945, just as the United States was beginning to develop its space program.

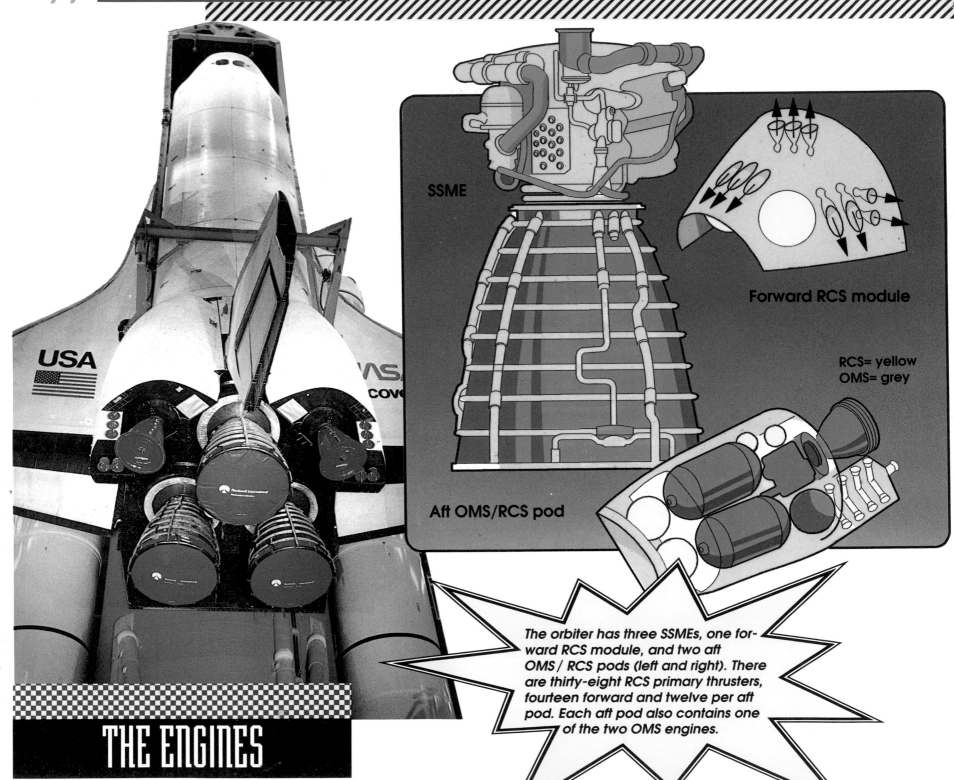

SSME

Forward RCS module

RCS= yellow
OMS= grey

Aft OMS/RCS pod

The orbiter has three SSMEs, one forward RCS module, and two aft OMS / RCS pods (left and right). There are thirty-eight RCS primary thrusters, fourteen forward and twelve per aft pod. Each aft pod also contains one of the two OMS engines.

THE ENGINES

more or less delicate work. The SRBs give us the big boost at liftoff. The main engines—known as SSMEs, for space shuttle main engines—power us through the atmosphere. Then once we're high enough, we use the OMS engines to insert ourselves into the proper orbit. And once we're in orbit, we can use the RCS engines to make precise adjustments and maneuver the orbiter. You'll find out soon enough that all of these propulsion systems are crucial. The main engines are too powerful for orbit corrections, and the RCS engines aren't powerful enough to get us off the launchpad."

"Flying the space shuttle seems pretty easy so far. If the computers do all the work, what's the difference between an astronaut and a passenger?"

Instantly, I see this was the wrong question to ask. Pilot looks like he's going to blow his top. "Easy? Do you have any idea what an enormous undertaking a shuttle mission is? Thousands of people work literally millions of man-hours to make this mission happen. And who do you think has to be ready to pilot the shuttle if something goes wrong?"

"Sorry." Just then CAPCOM breaks in with a message that doesn't sound good.

Discovery, Houston, we're showing an SSME *failure. Confirm.*

Pilot stops talking and stares at the computer screen in front of him. "Roger, Houston, we see it, too," he says. An eerie silence follows as we wait for orders. I'm too nervous to ask

what all the fuss is about. Finally, CAPCOM's voice returns.

Discovery, Houston, abort ATO. *Repeat, abort* ATO.

The pilot turns and looks daggers at me. "Roger, Houston," I say, "abort ATO." Then I turn to Pilot and ask the big question. "Abort WHAT?"

"Calm down. You're about to find out what all the astronaut training is for. We've lost a main engine, and Flight has called for an ATO. That's a type of intact abort."

"It doesn't sound very appealing."

"Maybe so, but it's a whole lot better than a contingency abort. If they'd called for a contingency, we'd be strapping on our parachutes now."

"You mean the mission is over, and we're returning to earth?"

"No. ATO stands for Abort to Orbit. Loss of a main engine is no picnic, but Flight thinks we're far enough into our ascent to push ahead for orbit. We'll figure out what the problem is when we get there."

"If we're heading into orbit anyway, why is this called an abort?"

"Because we'll be going into a lower orbit than was originally planned. Think of it as a holding pattern. If the situation turns out to be serious, we'll get the call to prepare for deorbit—meaning we're going home early. If not, we'll fire our OMS engines to boost us into a higher orbit. Anyway, what we have to do now is tell the shuttle's computers that we're in an ATO situation."

TRAINING

Space shuttle astronauts go through an exhaustive training program. Candidates for shuttle pilot, for example, are first trained as jet pilots, and each must log 1,000 hours of flying time. After they are selected to be part of the NASA team, astronaut trainees have to study astronomy, meteorology, computer science, and guidance and navigation theory, as well as other subjects related to space travel. Astronauts also train rigorously for the physical challenges of space, which mostly have to do with weightlessness.

Using a specially designed aircraft that simulates the effects of weightlessness, astronauts practice everyday chores like eating, drinking, and going to the bathroom. The Weightless Environment Training Facility—an enormous 25-foot-deep, water-filled tank—holds a full-scale model of the payload bay, where the astronauts prepare for the special mission tasks they will perform aboard the orbiter.

Using a series of steep climbs and dives, this NASA aircraft simulates zero gravity.

The final and most intensive period of training comes after an astronaut has been selected for a particular mission. During this time, the pilot and commander practice their roles endlessly in the space shuttle simulator at the Johnson Space Center. Strapped into an exact replica of the shuttle's cockpit, they run through the stages of liftoff, ascent, orbit, deorbit, and landing, while the simulator mimics all the motions and variables of a real space mission. At the same time, in Mission Control, the teams of experts who will be monitoring the actual flight also monitor the simulation, playing the same roles they will during the mission itself. A special team of trainers thinks up problems to throw at both the astronauts and the Mission Control teams to prepare them for unexpected eventualities. Typically, by launch day, first-time astronauts have spent so much time training that the actual mission feels like just another simulation.

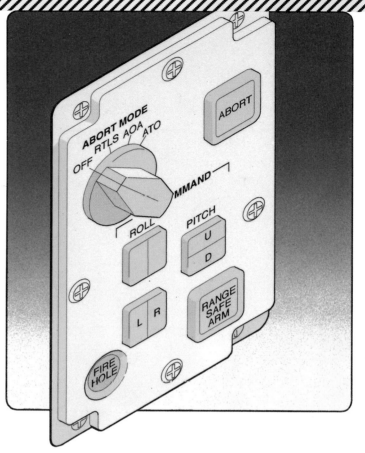

"O.K. How do we do that?"

"There's a rotary switch on your right-hand side marked ABORT. See it?"

"Roger. It's at OFF now. It's got settings marked RTLS, AOA, and ATO."

"Those are all types of aborts. We want an ATO abort, so turn the switch to ATO and then press the ABORT button."

"Roger."

"Good. Now we're in abort mode."

"What now?"

"Well, normally we'd have MECO—main engine cutoff—about eight and a half minutes after launch. But with one engine out, we'll

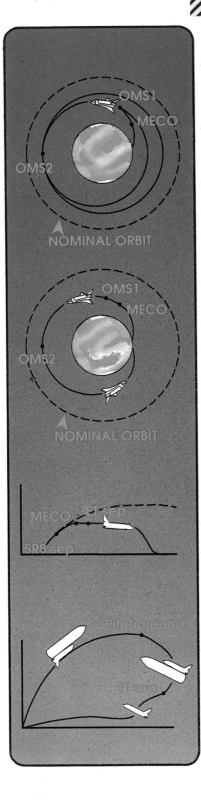

ABORT!

NASA has developed four different ways in which a shuttle mission can be aborted because of a serious malfunction like the loss of a main engine or a fuel tank leak. The flight director may choose one or another type of abort, depending on the type of malfunction and when it occurs.

ABORT TO ORBIT (ATO). This is the "best" type of abort because it means that the shuttle may still be able to continue its mission. An ATO is usually called for when a main engine fails within five to eight minutes after takeoff. In an ATO, the shuttle continues into space but goes into a lower orbit than the one planned. Once the shuttle achieves orbit, experts on the ground analyze the situation and decide whether the mission can continue or whether the shuttle must return to earth.

ABORT ONCE AROUND (AOA). This is the second best type of abort because it allows the shuttle to continue its ascent in a normal fashion. In an AOA, the shuttle makes one complete orbit before returning to earth.

TRANSATLANTIC LANDING (TAL). This type of abort is called for when a serious malfunction is discovered in the first three to seven minutes after takeoff. The shuttle never goes into orbit but instead takes on the characteristics of an airplane and flies across the Atlantic Ocean before landing at one of several designated emergency airstrips. The main TAL sites are located in Spain, Morocco, and Senegal.

RETURN TO LAUNCH SITE (RTLS). If a major systems failure is detected within the first three minutes of takeoff and the shuttle cannot reach a TAL site, it must try a return to the launch site. This is the riskiest type of abort because it involves several complicated and dangerous maneuvers. At one point during an RTLS abort, for instance, the shuttle must do a "pitcharound" and fly through the atmosphere backward in order to slow its velocity.

have to burn the other two longer and harder. Probably an extra thirty or sixty seconds."

A little less than a minute later, I feel another big bump. "Houston Discovery, we have nominal MECO," Pilot says. "'Nominal' is NASA's way of saying 'normal,'" he tells me.

Roger, Discovery, we see that, too.

"Now that we've cut off the main engines," Pilot explains, "we'll use the OMS engines to insert ourselves into orbit."

Suddenly I have the sensation that we've come to a complete stop. "What was that? Did we hit something?"

"Don't be silly," Pilot says. "There's nothing much up here to hit. We're a hundred miles above the earth."

"But we just stopped! Didn't you feel it?"

"We didn't stop. We just stopped *accelerating.* There's a difference between velocity and acceleration, you know. We're still speeding along at 25,000 feet per second, but our velocity is no longer increasing."

"We're going *how* fast?"

"It works out to about 17,000 miles per hour. You thought we had stopped because before we were accelerating at such a tremendous rate."

"You certainly seem pretty calm considering we just aborted." I mean this as a compliment, to make up for what I said before about astronauts not doing much.

"Astronauts spend a lot of time training for these situations," Pilot says coolly. "It becomes automatic."

"But this isn't training," I remind him. "This is real life." I notice a little bead of sweat on his upper lip now.

"Yes, that's true. But don't worry, pal. I'll get you through this. I'm an astronaut."

"Oh, right." Just as I say this, I hear an explosion, and the shuttle gives a nervous shake. "AGHHH! What was THAT?"

Discovery, Houston, ET sep.

"That's what it was," says Pilot. "ET sep. External tank separation. We just released the big external fuel tank."

"Wow. Where's it going?"

"Back to earth, of course."

"Lucky ET."

"Not really. It'll break up into a million pieces as it reenters the atmosphere."

"Oh. And where are we heading?"

"Out there. Space. The final frontier. We're on our way into orbit. Any second now we'll get the command to go for OMS burn."

"And what will that mean?"

"It'll mean we can fire the OMS engines, which will insert us into orbit. Once we're there..."

Discovery, Houston, OMS-1.

"Roger, Houston," I respond. "OMS-1." Then, to Pilot, I say, "Why is it called OMS-1?"

"To distinguish it from OMS-2, of course."

"Of course."

IN OUTER SPACE

Something strange begins to happen at this point, and I don't know what it is at first. My arms and legs, which until a minute ago

ACCELERATION

G-FORCE

ZERO GRAVITY

GRAVITY

Gravity is a force of attraction. As Isaac Newton noticed more than three hundred years ago, apples falling from a tree fall down, not up. That's because of the gravitational force that exists between each apple and the earth.

Gravitational force also exists between you and the apple, just as it does between any two objects. But the earth is much bigger than you are, so the attraction between it and the apple is much stronger.

Think of magnets, which always attract each other. Gravity works in the same way. The bigger the magnets, the stronger the force between them and the harder it is to pull them apart. Similarly, the bigger the objects, the stronger the gravitational force is between them. Gravity keeps the moon in orbit around the earth, and it also keeps the planets of the solar system revolving around the sun.

This same gravity is what holds the space shuttle to the launchpad. If enough thrust is applied in the opposite direction, however, the pull of the earth's gravity can be overcome. If you throw a ball straight up as hard as you can, at first it will rise quickly. But eventually it will slow down, stop momentarily, and then fall back to earth.

The force of gravity weakens quickly, however, as the distance between the two objects increases. So if you throw a ball with the force of a rocket engine, it will keep going until it has broken free of the earth's gravitational pull—and then it will keep going forever. The speed at which the ball—or any object, for that matter—would have to travel to escape the earth's gravity is called its escape velocity. The earth's escape velocity is 6.98 miles per second. On the moon, which has much less mass than the earth, the escape velocity is 1.5 miles per second.

seemed to weigh a hundred pounds each, suddenly feel as though they no longer want to remain attached to my body. I'd say they were trying to float upward, but I don't know which way is up anymore. Instead, I hold my arms out and whisper cautiously to Pilot, "Hey, look at this!"

"That's zero gravity. How does it feel?"

"Incredibly weird! What does zero gravity mean, exactly?"

"It means that your body isn't subject to the earth's gravitational pull anymore."

"But then . . . that must mean we're . . ." I turn left and look out my window ". . . in outer space!"

"Where did you think you'd find yourself? We're not in Kansas anymore, Commander, and we've got work to do."

I nod my head, but I can't take my eyes away from the window. Outside, there's empty blackness, but just below us, looking as wide and unending as an ocean, is the earth. "It seems so...so alive," I whisper. "It's huge. I expected it to be more distant. Like a little ball."

"The earth looks so big because we're in a low orbit. Any photos you may have seen were most likely taken by satellites in very high orbits, thousands of miles away. The shuttle normally flies at an orbit of about 160 miles. But since this is an ATO flight, we're in an even lower orbit than usual. Right now, we're orbiting at an altitude of 105 nautical miles."

"What next?" I ask Pilot.

"We have to prepare for OMS-2."

"Why do we need a second OMS burn?"

"In simple terms, we're in an egg-shaped orbit right now, and we want a perfect circle. To achieve that, we'll burn the OMS engines again when we reach the apogee of our orbit—that is, when our distance from the earth is at its greatest."

"Right. So how do we initiate OMS-2?"

"It's a complicated sequence. Better let me handle it."

Discovery, Houston, com check.

"Roger, Houston, we read you loud and clear," I sing out.

Roger, read you same, Discovery. We've checked on the SSME failure. We think the culprit might be a temperature sensor. We'll cross-check. Over.

"Roger, Houston," I say.

Discovery, Houston. You have a go for OMS-2.

"Roger, Houston," I reply. Then I keep quiet while Pilot flips through a notebook velcroed above him and enters commands into the computer. I figure it's a good idea not to disturb him at this point. "OMS-2 complete," Pilot says to me.

"Houston Discovery, OMS-2 complete," I call out.

Roger, Discovery. The residuals are O.K.

I give Pilot a sidelong look. "That means the OMS burn was sufficient to circularize our orbit," he says. "In other words, it worked."

Discovery, Houston, go for orbit OPS.

"Roger, Houston," I answer quickly. "Orbit OPS."

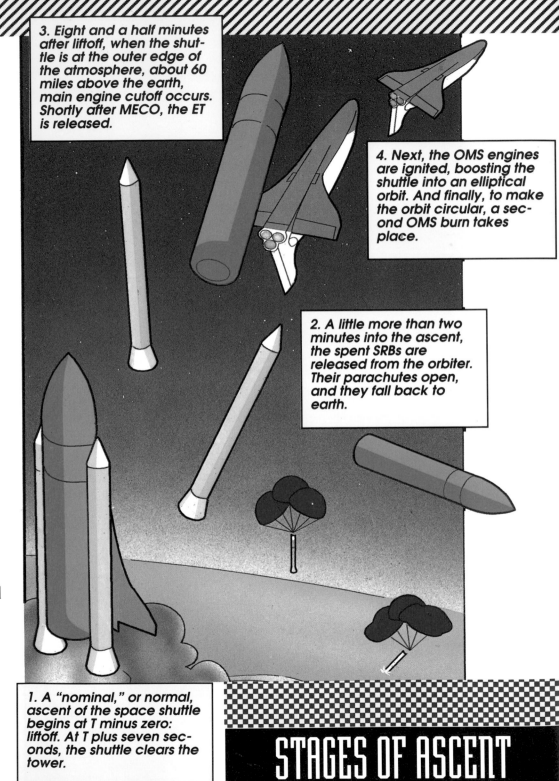

3. Eight and a half minutes after liftoff, when the shuttle is at the outer edge of the atmosphere, about 60 miles above the earth, main engine cutoff occurs. Shortly after MECO, the ET is released.

4. Next, the OMS engines are ignited, boosting the shuttle into an elliptical orbit. And finally, to make the orbit circular, a second OMS burn takes place.

2. A little more than two minutes into the ascent, the spent SRBs are released from the orbiter. Their parachutes open, and they fall back to earth.

1. A "nominal," or normal, ascent of the space shuttle begins at T minus zero: liftoff. At T plus seven seconds, the shuttle clears the tower.

STAGES OF ASCENT

ORBIT

"*A*ll right, Commander, it's time to load the orbit software. In other words, we can stay in orbit."

"Right. So what do I do?"

"You enter the commands using your keyboard. The program is called OPS 201-PRO. Got it?"

I key in the command very carefully. "Is that it?"

"That's it."

I expect bells to go off, but I don't hear anything except the collective buzz of the machinery.

"What did I just do?"

"You told the shuttle's computers that we've completed the ascent phase of the mission and entered the orbit phase. Now they'll replace the ascent software with the orbit software. All the software for running the shuttle's mission is stored in the computers' mass memory units, called MMUs for short. When you typed your command, the computers went to the MMUs and asked for the OPS-2 software."

"So, the software is broken into two parts?"

"Actually, there are three main programs. OPS-1 is the ascent software, which is further broken down into subprograms, called major modes, or MMs. MM101 controls prelaunch and liftoff. MM102 takes over at liftoff and runs through the first stage of ascent, ending with the command to release the solid rocket boosters. MM103 runs the next stage of the flight, ending at MECO. MM104 brings us to the OMS-1 burn. MM105 is the program that controls the OMS-2 burn that circularizes our orbit. So you see, each stage of the ascent is controlled by a different software program. Then, after the ascent software, comes the orbit software, OPS-2, which you just loaded. The third major program, OPS-3, carries out the reentry-and-landing phase of the mission."

"You talk about the shuttle's computers as though they were on board. It seems to me that it would take a whole roomful of computers to control this baby. Aren't they on the ground?"

THE COMPUTERS

Nearly every part of the space shuttle's mission is controlled or monitored by a computer. There are five general purpose computers on board. Four of these are the primary computers. The fifth is a backup. The GPCs are surprisingly small: 19.55 inches long by 7.62 inches high by 10.2 inches wide. Each weighs 64 pounds.

Software for navigation and systems management is divided among the four primary GPCs, but any one of the computers could navigate the mission if the others failed. And if all four primary computers failed, the backup would take over.

To guard against design flaws in the software, NASA hired two companies to create the shuttle's computer programs. IBM designed and coded the primary system software, and Rockwell developed the backup software.

"No, they're right here with us. In fact, each of the five general purpose computers, or GPCs, is only about as big as a dresser drawer."

"You're not serious."

"I am. And get this: any one of those five computers is capable of running almost the entire mission by itself."

"Then why have five of them?"

"Redundancy. That's a byword in the space shuttle program. It means repetition of systems. There are at least two ways to do every task on board, and often there are four or five. The point is to protect against unknowns, such as breakdowns, leaks, and equipment failures. That's why we have two OMS engines. And why there are backup control systems. Do you remember, for instance, how you programmed the abort mode?"

"I turned the switch and pressed the ABORT button."

"Right. But what would you have done if that switch had broken off in your hand as you were turning it?"

"Glued it back on?"

"No, you would have communicated the ATO command to the computer using the keyboard. You see? There are at least two ways to do everything."

Discovery, Houston. Confirm temperature sensor is the culprit on the SSME shutdown. Over.

"Is that good or bad?" I ask Pilot, but I can tell the answer from the look of relief on his face.

"It's very good. It means that the engine shut down because the computer told it to, and the computer told it to because it thought the engine was overheating."

"But it wasn't?"

"No, there's no problem with the SSMEs, just with the sensor. We'll probably get the order soon to do another burn."

Discovery, Houston. You have a go for OMS burn to orbit at 135. Over.

"Roger, Houston," I say. "OMS burn to 135."

After a few moments of flipping switches and punching information into the keyboard, we hear a boom and feel the OMS engines lurch us forward. The ride up to the higher orbit of 135 nautical miles is remarkably smooth compared to the ride through the atmosphere. I mention this to Pilot.

"Sure," he says. "After all, the space shuttle is now operating in space. Getting through the earth's atmosphere was a big drag, pardon the pun. But now it's smooth sailing from here on."

"So now we're in a nominal orbit, huh?"

"That's right. Now we can get down to business." But it wasn't Pilot who said this. I turn around and find two astronauts—a man and a woman—seated behind me. They both nod hello.

"Have you two been here all this time?"

"Of course we've been here."

Pilot introduces them. "Meet our mission specialists. They have the overall responsibility for onboard operations, such as monitoring the life support systems, conducting experiments, and handling deployments."

"But right now let's get out of these monkey suits." And with that, the pair of them snap off their helmets and unzip their flight suits. The next thing I know, the mission specialists are standing—or rather floating—in blue cotton shorts and T-shirts.

"During liftoff, the two of us let you fly boys do your job. Now that we're in orbit, though, it's our turn to take the lead," explains the female mission specialist. "We have to check on the cargo bay, prepare the experiments, and get ready for all the other work that's to be done on this mission."

Discovery, Houston. You have a go to continue the mission. Try to get some rest, folks. That was a close one.

"You can say that again, Houston," I respond. Pilot and I both give a sigh of relief. "Even though I didn't do much, that was exhausting work," I say.

"Not knowing whether there's a major problem can take a lot out of you," Pilot agrees. "Fortunately, we're coming up on presleep."

"I like the sound of that."

"Presleep is personal time. It's the designated two-hour period before the lights go out when every astronaut gets to relax. You can read, play chess, do whatever. Most of us like to plug in our headphones, listen to music, and watch the earth through the windows."

"That sounds nice. But I don't know how relaxed I can get in this cramped seat."

"So unbuckle yourself. You aren't trapped in the cockpit. Everybody has full run of the orbiter. But before we go down to the mid deck and meet the rest of the crew, there's an important task we have to take care of. One of the first things we always do when we reach orbit is open the payload bay doors. That cools the life support systems and keeps the machinery from overheating. To start the procedure, find the switch on aft panel R13 marked PL BAY DOOR. Then turn it to the open position."

"O.K., I did it. Anything else?"

"That's all. The computer does the rest, and the mission and payload specialists monitor everything. If you look out the rear windows, you can watch the doors open. Each of the two doors is 60 feet long, and the payload bay itself is big enough to hold a school bus."

Once the doors are open, we float down the hatch at the back of the cockpit to the next level. There, two more astronauts

Shuttle Payload Bay

introduce themselves as payload specialists. The payload specialists, I learn, have come along to monitor the satellite that is scheduled to be placed in orbit. We chat for a while, then everyone goes off to a different corner of the mid deck for some privacy. Pilot hands me a tape player and asks what kind of music I like.

"What have you got?"

"Take your pick—from Mozart to heavy metal."

I spend the next hour or so listening to a Mozart symphony while the earth spins past my window. Then I rejoin the rest of the crew, who are strapping themselves into sleeping bags. Something is definitely strange about the sleeping arrangements. "Why are some of the sleeping bags attached to the walls?" I ask.

"Think about it," Pilot says. "Because there's no gravity here, there's no up or down. So it doesn't matter whether you sleep lying on the floor or the wall or the ceiling. It's all the same." "Wow. I think this will take some getting used to." But as soon as I'm safely strapped in—so that I don't go floating away—I forget all about the fact that I'm lying down on a wall. I close my eyes, and the astonishing, giddy, nervous ride into space fades away.

A DAY IN SPACE

"Good morning, Commander!" I open my eyes and see Pilot floating in front of me. "Did you sleep well?"

"I guess so," I answer. "How long was I out?"

"Eight hours exactly. Have some breakfast now before we get back to work. Houston will be wanting to get things rolling soon."

At that precise moment, a blast of music rocks the compartment. It's loud, it's funky, it's Ray Charles. Then comes the voice of CAPCOM.

A *very good morning to you, Discovery crew members!*

""It's sort of a tradition that Mission Control wakes us up with music," Pilot tells me. "Hope you don't mind."

After a quick breakfast of cereal, freeze-dried eggs, and freeze-dried coffee sucked through a straw, I'm ready for the day's work. Pilot and I return to our seats in the cockpit—mine on the left side, Pilot's on the right—and we strap ourselves down. Just then, I turn to Pilot and frown.

"I'm really sorry, but is there time for me to run—or float—to the bathroom?"

"Sure," he chuckles. "But have someone show you how to use the toilet. It takes some getting used to."

I return several minutes later, shaking my head. "That's a pretty wild toilet you have."

"Yes, well, the problem is zero gravity. You have to keep the waste from floating up out of the bowl, so the toilet comes with an air suction system. Pulling the handle up closes a valve that traps the waste. Pushing the handle forward opens another gate valve that exposes the toilet bowl to the cold darkness of space. The vacuum outside sucks the oxygen out of the toilet and, in effect, freeze-dries the waste."

"Working it isn't the easiest thing in the world, but I think I managed. So, what's our first task?"

Before Pilot can answer, though, he's interrupted by the day's first official call from Mission Control, and it's a strange one.

Discovery Houston. Prepare for Zone of Exclusion.

I turn quickly to Pilot. "Is that where we meet the Klingons?"

"They're referring to a communications blackout," he says, ignoring my joke. "The ZOE is the area in which we can't receive any signals."

"You mean we're about to be cut off? But we just started the day."

"True, but these things can't be helped, and it won't be for long. We're able to maintain communications for about 90 percent of the time in orbit."

"What happens the rest of the time? Do we go behind a cloud or something?"

"No, it has to do with the way the tracking system is set up. Communication is possible thanks to the Tracking and Data Relay Satellite System, called TDRSS or tee-dris. TDRSS consists of two satellites sitting about 22,000 miles over the equator, one in the middle of the Pacific Ocean and the other off the east coast of South America."

"Why place the satellites there?"

"They have to be within range of the ground station in New Mexico. As it is, they're located at either extreme of that range. There's an area of overlap for which both satellites can provide a communications link. But there's also a gap in the coverage on the opposite side of the globe. Still, it's a vast improvement over the old days when astronauts in space were only in contact with the earth about 20 percent of the time."

"So I guess we just play checkers or something while we're in the ZOE."

The shuttle enters the Zone of Exclusion.

"Well, that's up to you. You see, the person officially in charge of the shuttle's mission is the flight director. The one exception comes during communications blackouts, when the shuttle's commander has total authority. All problems that arise are his or hers to deal with."

"Oh, great. So you're throwing everything onto my shoulders, is that it?"

"I'm not throwing anything. I'm just telling you the rules. But don't worry. I'll get you through this."

Just as I'm about to rule that the blackout time be spent gazing out the windows, I hear a sound very much like a fire alarm. "What on earth is that?"

Pilot is staring fiercely at the screen in front of him. I look at my screen. It says: O_2 FLOW, N_2 FLOW.

"Really weird!" Pilot mutters. I'm not used to him speaking in street talk, and it doesn't make me feel very relaxed. "Hit your alarm button!" he says. I press the red ALARM button, and the siren shuts off. "We're losing oxygen and nitrogen fast. And I have no idea why."

"Is it serious?" I ask.

"Of course it's serious. At this rate, we could lose all our oxygen in a matter of hours."

"Houston, Discovery!" I call. "Houston, this is the space shuttle Discovery. Do you read me? Jeez Louise, we're in trouble here!"

"What's wrong with you?" Pilot growls. "We're in a blackout, remember? They can't hear you."

"Oh, great. Here we are, lost in the Zone of Exclusion, watching all our oxygen blow away. What am I supposed to do?"

"First of all, get hold of yourself. We're not lost. We just have to figure out what's causing the problem. Now, why would oxygen from our storage tanks be flowing into the cabin?"

"Hmmmmm. Could it be because somewhere else the oxygen is flowing out?"

Pilot turns to me with a look of respect. It seems strange because this is the first time I've seen it. "A leak! Of course!"

He starts flipping switches and punching commands into his keypad. "I'm trying to zero in on it," he explains. This goes on for several

TRACKING SYSTEM

Communicating with a ship traveling 150 miles above the earth at a speed of 17,000 miles per hour is no easy task. The key is the Tracking and Data Relay Satellite System, or TDRSS. When Mission Control wants to send a message to the shuttle, the communication first goes to the satellite ground station at White Sands, New Mexico. From there, it's beamed up to one of the two TDRSS satellites. The satellite then relays the signal back down to the shuttle, which is orbiting at a much lower altitude.

In order for the TDRSS system to work, the two satellites must stay in the same relative positions above the earth, in what is called a geosynchronous orbit. Because of the pull of gravity, the lower a satellite's altitude, the faster it will orbit around the earth. At an altitude of 150 miles, the space shuttle takes 90 minutes to complete each revolution. At an altitude of 22,300 miles, however, the TDRSS satellites take exactly 24 hours to make one revolution, a speed that precisely matches the earth's own rotation.

minutes, and then we hear a voice that makes me want to weep with joy.

Discovery, Houston, com check.

"Roger, Houston, we read you!" I shout. "And, hey, we've got a problem up here."

Roger, Discovery, we copy. We've got the same message down here, and we're trying to confirm the leak.

"It's for real, Houston," I say. "We've been trying to isolate it."

Well, if you don't find and stop it within ten minutes, we'll be forced to scrub the mission and call you folks home. Over.

Pilot is shaking his head, which I don't like. "I just don't understand why the leak isn't registering anywhere," he says. "I mean, how could you possibly have oxygen blowing out of the orbiter and not know where the leak is?"

Just then a light bulb pops on in my head. "Hey, Pilot, I know this might sound crazy, but—you remember you told me that the toilet sucks oxygen out of the bowl? Well, I did have a little trouble..."

"Commander, you're a genius!" Pilot cries.

Within two minutes, we've zeroed in on the problem. The valve that is supposed to seal off the inner chamber of the toilet somehow jammed open when I used it. So all the oxygen in the cabin has been rushing out through the toilet and into space. Our mission specialists jump on the problem and, using an ordinary pair of pliers, force the valve shut. Instantly, the cabin pressure starts to climb back into the normal range. Then we get the seal of approval from Mission Control.

Discovery, Houston. All systems nominal.

"Whew! That's one situation I hope never happens again," Pilot says. "Now we can get back to the business at hand."

"Which is?"

"Deployment, of course. Our payload for this mission is a research satellite for the European space agency."

"Why is it called a payload, anyway?"

"Because it pays for the mission. The shuttle program isn't simply a research and development deal paid for by our tax dollars. We're also a business. We're a package delivery and pickup service, a kind of Pony Express in space."

"What do you mean by pickup?"

"Shuttles don't just deploy satellites. Sometimes we pick up ailing ones, repair them, and send them back on their way."

"O.K., what do we do first?"

"We take out the Flight Data File and follow it, step by step. The file details everything we're responsible for on this mission. To launch this particular payload, we first have to put the orbiter through a series of positional maneuvers. The satellite we're carrying has its own tracking system, which tells it where it is. Before we release it, though, we've got to make sure that its tracking system is aligned with ours."

"Does that mean we're going to steer with these joysticks here?"

"They're called controllers, and no, we're not going to steer with them. All the maneuvers are performed by the computers."

"Oh. Of course." I feel a kick at this point. "Hey! What was that?"

"Those were the large RCS rockets firing."

"I thought the RCS was for fine-tuned movements. That felt like we were blindsided by a bull."

"Everything is relative. The larger RCS rockets each have 870 pounds of thrust. That's what we just felt. Most of the time, though, it's the smaller, 24-pound thrusters that fire. They don't have nearly the kick."

"Commander, we're all set to go here." I turn around. It's one of the payload specialists talking to me.

"Roger," I say. Then: "Houston, Discovery, we're ready to deploy."

Roger, Discovery. You're go to deploy.

Turning to Pilot, I mouth the words "Now what?" He smiles and points to the window. "Just watch," he says.

Outside is one of the most remarkable views I could imagine. With the payload bay doors wide open, I can see the satellite being lifted from its nest by the mission specialists working at the aft control station. The wide curve of the earth floats above the bay, and there's a long, thin arm silhouetted against it. The arm is clamped down on the satellite, and it's unfolding as the satellite moves outward.

SATELLITE DEPLOYMENT

"What's with the arm?" I ask.

"That's the Remote Manipulator System," Pilot explains. "But it's O.K. to call it the arm. It's our primary means of moving payloads around in space. As you can see, it has three joints, which you might think of as a shoulder, an elbow, and a wrist."

By now, the arm is fully extended and holding the satellite out into space.

Looks good, Discovery. You're go for release.

"Roger, Houston," I reply. "O.K., folks, go for release."

And with that, the arm lets go, and the satellite floats slowly, slowly away from us, backing steadily into the darkness of deep space.

Pilot nudges me. "Call 'sep 1,'" he says.

"Houston, Discovery, sep 1."

Roger, Discovery. Looks like a great release and sep 1. Congratulations.

We all break out in a round of spontaneous applause, pleased and relieved that the most important phase of our mission has gone off successfully.

"Now what do we do?" I ask Pilot. "Listen to Mozart and watch the earth rotate?"

"Not so fast, Commander. This isn't an amusement ride. Each shuttle mission costs over $100 million, and NASA wants to get the most for its money. Right now, the mission specialists are setting up experiments in the mid deck. While they do that, our job is to monitor the orbiter's systems and keep it flying smoothly."

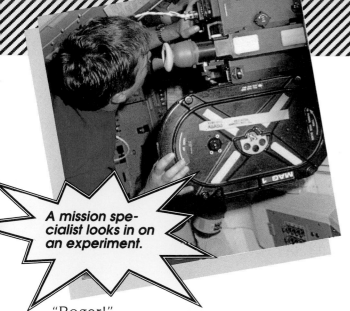

A mission specialist looks in on an experiment.

"Roger!"

And we set about correcting the orbit and monitoring just about everything under the sun:

• the purge, vent, and drain system, which flushes hazardous gases out of the cavities in the orbiter where they may accumulate;

• the orbital maneuvering system, our primary source of thrust now that the main engines have been cut off;

• the life support systems, which include cabin temperature controls, the supply water and waste water systems, and waste management;

• the avionics, or aviation electronics, system, which includes the general purpose computers, the main memory units, and the 300 miles of wiring that tie the computers into every part of the ship.

We take turns at each task, so there is time left over for me to observe some of the scientific experiments on the mid deck. The day is full of things to do, not the least of which is pretending that this is a normal day despite the fact that the sun rises and sets every 90 minutes as we fly around the earth. By the end of the day, what with all the activity and the strangeness of space, I'm ready to climb into my sleeping bag and hit the wall. And that's just what I do.

LEAVING ORBIT

Swing low, sweet chariot,
Coming for to carry me home

That's the wake-up call on the final morning of the mission. We've been up here a week now, and every morning it's been something different: Madonna, Beethoven, Tony Bennett. The folks at Mission Control have far-ranging musical tastes.

By now I've gotten pretty good at monitoring the RCS jets, and CAPCOM and I are like old pals. I'm even used to the sixteen sunrises and sixteen sunsets we get every twenty-four hours. But it's time to prepare for landing, and I have to admit that I'm pretty excited.

"Everything stowed?" I ask the crew. "Payload bay doors shut? Tools packed away?" Pilot and I go down the checklist of things to do before deorbit. Then we strap ourselves into our seats in the cockpit.

Discovery, Houston.

"Go ahead, Houston."

Roger. You're go for deorbit burn. Conditions at Edwards Air Force Base are good. We're looking at a touchdown at 195 knots.

"Roger, Houston," I say. "Go for deorbit burn."

I don't have to look at Pilot for an explanation because he's already told me about the deorbit burn. It comes when we leave orbit and are about to reenter the earth's atmosphere. Right away, however, something strange seems to be happening. "Pilot, is it my imagination or are we doing a one-eighty?"

"You've got it right, Commander."

"But what's the point of entering the atmosphere in reverse? Isn't that dangerous?"

"Don't worry. After the deorbit burn, we'll maneuver the orbiter back to its proper nose-first attitude before we hit the atmo-sphere. But now the point is to decrease our speed. We're using the RCS engines to position ourselves tail first. Then we'll fire the OMS engines, which will act as a kind of brake. Slowing the orbiter down by firing the OMS engines in reverse is called retrofiring. We plot a change in velocity, and that change is called the deorbit delta V. The delta (Δ), a Greek letter, often stands for change in scientific measures, and the V stands for velocity.

Our deorbit delta V today is about 350 feet per second."

"You mean this maneuver will slow us down by 350 feet per second?"

"That's right. But when you think about it in perspective, it's not so much. After all, right now we're flying at about 25,000 feet per second. If the deorbit delta V decreases that by 350 feet per second, what are we left with?"

"Uhhhh . . . that would be 24,650 feet per second."

"Not much of a change, right? So what do you think will take away the rest of that velocity?"

"An emergency brake?"

"Very funny. No, we have another kind of brake—the earth's atmosphere. The deorbit burn slows us just enough so that we drop back down into the atmosphere."

"Wait a second. You mean the atmosphere slows us down?"

"Of course it does. I told you that the atmosphere was a big drag, right? It exerts tremendous friction on the ship, and that friction slows us down. The tricky part, though, is figuring out exactly how much atmosphere we have to travel through to dissipate our speed. Fortunately, the computers make that calculation for us."

"Do you mean to tell me that the computers, sitting in space halfway around the world from the landing site, can figure out how much atmosphere we have to travel through to land safely?"

STS-32
DEORBIT & REENTRY TRACK

DEORBIT PREBURN MANEUVER

DEORBIT POSTBURN MANEUVER

DEORBIT BURN

INITIATE ENTRY GUIDANCE MAJOR MODE 304

ENTRY INTERFACE

HAWAII

INITIATE TACTICAL AIR NAVIGATION (TACAN) UPDATING

LONGITUDE, DEGREES

Rockwell International
Space Transportation
Systems Division

"That's exactly what I'm telling you. It's amazing, isn't it? You see, we've got no engines on reentry. We're like a big glider barreling down at incredible speed. Of course, there are variations in atmospheric density and wind speed, which the computers can't measure exactly from here. But they come awfully close, and to make up any difference, we'll do a series of S-turns as necessary to lose more speed. Those S-turns also prevent too much heat from building up."

"We seem to be headfirst again."

"Right. The pitcharound is complete, and we're heading on course."

I look out my window and see the surface of the shuttle glowing red-hot. Turning to the overhead window, I see what looks like a flame that keeps building and collapsing.

"Holy cow! We're on fire!"

"Don't be alarmed. That's supposed to happen. What you're seeing is an envelope of gas particles that ignite as we bite into the atmosphere. We just went from an external temperature of -300°F in deep space to 6,000°F on reentry. That's why the tiles that form the shuttle's skin are so important."

I watch the glowing subside as we continue down into the atmosphere. "Hey, we're in blue sky!"

THE SHUTTLE'S SKIN

The tiles that shield the shuttle from the extreme temperatures of space are made out of a common earth material, sand. The sand is processed into fibers, making the finished product extremely light-weight because it's 90 percent air.

The tiles are then covered with a protective coating and attached to the shuttle with a material known at NASA as vulcanizing adhesive (but known in hardware stores as bath-room caulk). This high-tech skin made from low-tech ingredients forms the perfect protection for space travelers.

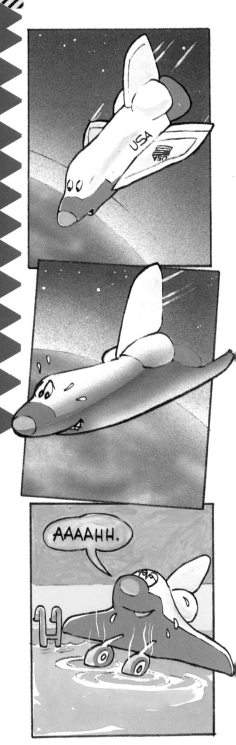

Discovery, Houston, we have a nominal entry. You're passing through Mach 5. Over.

"Roger, read you, Houston. Nominal entry." I turn to Pilot. "Sorry, what is Mach 5? Is that our speed?"

"Right. The Mach number is the ratio of our speed to the speed of sound. In other words, Houston was clocking us at five times the speed of sound. But now, if you look at the indicators, you'll see that we're inside Mach 3, or three times the speed of sound. Why don't you do a readings check?"

"Houston, Discovery," I call. "Our altitude is

75,000 feet. We're descending at 163 feet per second. We're 145 nautical miles from home. Over."

Discovery, Houston. Roger, read you. Ground track and nav are go.

"O.K., Commander, our speed is just about subsonic now. How about taking over the controls?"

I look at Pilot. I've been practicing this for several days now, and I feel ready. I take the hand controller and nod. We're in manual now, and I'm going to steer us in.

"Now, remember," Pilot says, "you have three possible movements at your disposal: pitch, roll, and yaw. Each one describes turning on a different axis. You pitch the orbiter, or bring its nose up or down, by pulling back and pushing forward on the control. To yaw—that is, move right or left—swivel the controller clockwise or counterclockwise. To bank the orbiter for a turn, or roll, drop the wings by tilting the controller to the right or left."

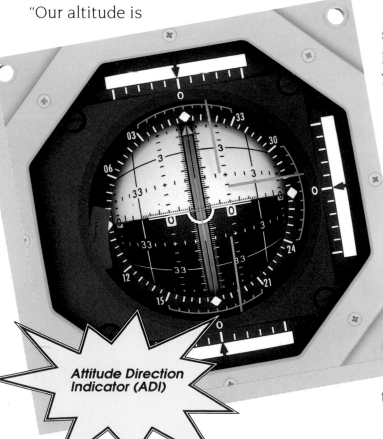

Attitude Direction Indicator (ADI)

Changes of direction are indicated on a rolling ball display. Pitching the orbiter rolls the ball up or down. Yawing the orbiter rotates the ball left or right. Rolling the orbiter spins the ball clockwise or counterclockwise.

COMING HOME

"So what do I do?"

"Hold it steady as she goes. We're still getting readings from the computer, which I'll relay to you as needed."

"Roger. Steady as she goes."

Discovery, we see you on energy approaching the HAC. You look in great shape.

"Roger, Houston. Thanks."

"The computers still say we have to dissipate a bit of energy," Pilot tells me. "I want you to roll her left."

"Roger." I tilt the controller slightly left, and our left wing dips.

"Great. Now bring her back up. You should sight along the HAC now."

"The what? The what?"

"Don't be so jumpy. The HAC is the heading alignment cylinder. It's the circle that has just been superimposed on your entry display."

Discovery, on glide slope, on centerline.

"Roger," I say. "What did that mean, Pilot?"

"Never mind. It means you're doing a great job. We're just one minute to touchdown now, 5.5 nautical miles out. Altitude 4,300 feet. Altitude 4,000 feet. Altitude 3,700 feet. Velocity Mach .5 and slowing."

"Jeez! The runway looks awfully hard. What if I can't..."

"Don't say that. Just watch your line, Commander. Easy does it. Four hundred feet. Three hundred. Two hundred. Landing gear down and locked. No! Don't pitch the nose down now or we'll touch nosegear first and

flip over. That's it. Keep it steady. Excellent! Main landing gear touchdown. And...nosegear touchdown! Great job, Commander!"

We come to a complete stop, and I'm covered with perspiration. "Wow! That was the hardest part of the flight." Then something occurs to me. I suddenly feel very wise. "You know, Pilot, it's really amazing how the computers run the whole mission. But even with all their sophistication, they can't steer us down onto the runway. I guess that means there's just no replacement for good old human skill, huh?"

Pilot pauses for a second, then gives me a grin. "Well, to tell you the truth, the computers could have flown us all the way in. Our landing software is nearly perfect. But I thought you'd prefer to do it yourself."

I can't help feeling deflated by this news. "But there must be *something* humans can do that computers can't."

"There is. We can laugh. And it's a whole lot more entertaining to watch a human flying the space shuttle than a computer."

With that remark comes the final message from Mission Control.

Discovery, Houston. Mission accomplished. Well done, Commander.

GLOSSARIZED INDEX

X-ray Vision Series

Each title in the series is 8½" × 11", 48 pages, with four-color photographs and illustrations.

Looking Inside the Brain
Ron Schultz
$9.95 paper

Looking Inside Cartoon Animation
Ron Schultz
$9.95 paper

Looking Inside Sports Aerodynamics
Ron Schultz
$9.95 paper

The Quill Hedgehog Adventures Series

G reen fiction for young readers. Each title in the series is written by John Waddington-Feather and illustrated by Doreen Edmond.

Quill's Adventures in the Great Beyond
Book One
5½" × 8½", 96 pages, $5.95 paper

Quill's Adventures in Wasteland
Book Two
5½" × 8½", 132 pages, $5.95 paper

Quill's Adventures in Grozzieland
Book Three
5½" × 8½", 132 pages, $5.95 paper

Masters of Motion Series

Each title in the series is 10¼" × 9", 48 pages, with four-color photographs and illustrations.

How to Drive an Indy Race Car
David Rubel
$9.95 paper

How to Fly a 747
Tim Paulson
$9.95 paper

How to Fly the Space Shuttle
Russell Shorto
$9.95 paper   (avail. 11/92)

The Extremely Weird Series

A ll of the titles in the Extremely Weird Series are written by Sarah Lovett, are 8½" × 11", 48 pages, and $9.95 paperbacks.

Extremely Weird Bats

Extremely Weird Birds

Extremely Weird Endangered Species

Extremely Weird Fishes

Extremely Weird Frogs

Extremely Weird Insects

Extremely Weird Primates

Extremely Weird Reptiles

Extremely Weird Sea Creatures

Extremely Weird Spiders

Other Titles of Interest

Kids Explore America's Hispanic Heritage
Westridge Young Writers Workshop
7" × 9", 112 pages, illustrations
$7.95 paper

Rads, Ergs, and Cheeseburgers
The Kids' Guide to Energy and the Environment
Bill Yanda
Illustrated by Michael Taylor
7" × 9", 108 pages, two-color illustrations
$12.95 paper

The Kids' Environment Book
What's Awry and Why
Anne Pedersen
Illustrated by Sally Blakemore
7" × 9", 192 pages, two-color illustrations
$13.95 paper
For Ages 10 and Up

The Indian Way
Learning to Communicate with Mother Earth
Gary McLain
Paintings by Gary McLain
Illustrations by Michael Taylor
7" × 9", 114 pages, two-color illustrations
$9.95 paper

The Kidding Around Travel Series

A ll of the titles listed below are 64 pages and $9.95 except for *Kidding Around the National Parks of the Southwest* and *Kidding Around Spain*, which are 108 pages and $12.95.

Kidding Around Atlanta

Kidding Around Boston

Kidding Around Chicago

Kidding Around the Hawaiian Islands

Kidding Around London

Kidding Around Los Angeles

Kidding Around the National Parks of the Southwest

Kidding Around New York City

Kidding Around Paris

Kidding Around Philadelphia

Kidding Around San Diego

Kidding Around San Francisco

Kidding Around Santa Fe

Kidding Around Seattle

Kidding Around Spain

Kidding Around Washington, D.C.

ORDERING INFORMATION Your books will be sent to you via UPS (for U.S. destinations). UPS will not deliver to a P.O. Box; please give us a street address. Include $3.75 for the first item ordered and $.50 for each additional item to cover shipping and handling costs. For airmail within the U.S., enclose $4.00. All foreign orders will be shipped surface rate; please enclose $3.00 for the first item and $1.00 for each additional item. Please inquire about foreign airmail rates.

METHOD OF PAYMENT Your order may be paid by check, money order, or credit card. We cannot be responsible for cash sent through the mail. All payments must be made in U.S. dollars drawn on a U.S. bank. Canadian postal money orders in U.S. dollars are acceptable. For VISA, MasterCard, or American Express orders, include your card number, expiration date, and your signature, or call (800) 888-7504. Books ordered on American Express cards can be shipped only to the billing address of the cardholder. Sorry, no C.O.D.'s. Residents of sunny New Mexico, add 5.875% tax to the total.

Address all orders and inquiries to: **John Muir Publications**, P.O. Box 613, Santa Fe, NM 87504, (505) 982-4078, (800) 888-7504.